my little Treasury
Cuddle Up Stories

publications international, ltd.

Contents

Four Friends

Illustrated by Cathy Johnson

Cat, Bird, Snake, and Turtle were four best friends who got in an argument one day.

"I hear that the houses in the city are as tall as mountains," said short-legged Turtle.

"No," said high-soaring Bird," the houses in the city are like little boxes."

"Maybe some are like mountains and some are like boxes," said curious Cat.

"Or mountains that are boxes," said slithery Snake.

The four friends argued until the next day, when they decided to see the houses for themselves.

They began the long journey to the city much in the same way as they had begun that day, by stretching their muscles and disagreeing. They walked and argued for days.

"Mountains!"

"Boxes!"

"Mountains and boxes!"

"Mountain boxes!"

"I've got to go back," said Cat one day. "I am very thirsty and I cannot find my water bowl."

"We'll go on," said the others. "You can catch up once you find it."

Several days later, they passed a palm-nut tree.

"I'm hungry," said Bird. "I want to eat some nuts."

"It will be a long time before those nuts are ripe," said Turtle and Snake. But Bird decided to stay until the nuts were ready to eat.

After many more days, Snake and Turtle came to a branch that lay across the road. Snake slithered right over it, but Turtle's legs were too short to climb over.

"I don't want to leave you," Snake said, "but I want to see the city." So Snake left Turtle behind.

Snake then grew hungry and decided to eat. His friends would have warned him that snakes cannot move for a long time after eating a meal, had they been there with him. But soon Snake had a full belly and could only lie on the road.

Snake was lonely, and he lost track of the time as he digested his meal. He thought so much about his friends who were far away that he forgot about the houses in the city.

Each friend was alone for a long time, but eventually, Cat found her water bowl, Bird ate the ripened palm nuts, and Turtle got past the tree branch.

Soon Snake began to move again, too. As he slithered along, he looked up and saw Bird. She swooped down and carried Snake in her talons. The two friends were so happy to see each other that they forgot to argue. After a short while, they saw Cat, with Turtle riding on her back.

Together, the four friends finally made it to the city. They saw that the houses were neither as tall as mountains nor as small as boxes.

"Oh, no!" said Cat. "We were all wrong."

"Maybe so," said Turtle, "but we found something else very important."

"Yes…," said Bird.

"We found each other!" said Snake.

Mom's Hot Chocolate

Original poem written by Joanna Spathis
Illustrated by Margie Moore

Her kitchen is toasty,
    and she has set out some mugs
Filled with creamy, warm chocolate,
    as warm as her hugs!

It is rarely too hot
    and never too cold.
But what makes it best—
    or so I am told—

Is that, besides the chocolate,
    and a marshmallow or two,
She makes it with love
    and especially for you!

16

I Love You

Original poem written by Julia Lobo
Illustrated by Janet Samuel

I love you, I love you,
   my sweet little bear.
Running and laughing,
   we don't have a care.

I hide and you find me,
   and then it's your turn.
Playing together,
   there's so much to learn.

I love you, my darling,
　　my sweet bunny dear.
Close by my side,
　　you have nothing to fear.

Now out in the meadow,
　　it's time for a treat.
We'll find some carrots
　　and berries to eat.

My sweet little joey,
    I love you so much.
I give you kisses
    and nuzzles and such.

With cuddles and snuggles,
    I hold you so tight.
You're in my arms now,
    to my heart's delight.

23

24

I love you, my baby,
    my elephant friend.
Time for your bath now—
    the fun doesn't end.

I'll wash you and dry you,
    my dear little one.
Showers and splashes
    make your bath time fun.

I love you, I love you,
    my birdies so sweet.
It sounds just like music
    whenever you tweet.

It's time for a story,
    to finish up our fun—
Come listen, gather round,
    get cuddly, everyone.

27

A Fish for You

There once was a fish.
    What more could you wish?
He lived in the sea.
    Where else would he be?
He was caught on a line.
    Whose line if not mine?
So I brought him to you.
    What else should I do?

Stone Soup

Adapted by Mary Rowitz
Illustrated by Sharron O'Neil

A hungry traveler had been roaming the countryside for a long time, and he hadn't eaten a good meal in quite a while. One day, the traveler spotted a lovely village off in the distance. He became very excited.

"I'm bound to find someone in the village who will share a meal with me," he thought.

As the hungry traveler hurried to the town, he tripped over a stone in the road. The stone was not like any he had ever seen before. It was perfectly smooth and oval in shape, and it fit perfectly in his paw. The traveler looked at the stone carefully and decided he would keep it.

"You never know when a stone like this might come in handy," he said.

Then the hungry traveler happily headed to the village. His empty stomach grumbled as he walked.

When the traveler arrived in the village, things did not go as well as he had hoped. He stopped at a few houses but had no luck finding a meal. One of the villagers was even quite grumpy. But the hungry traveler did not give up. The next house he came to was very quiet. The hungry traveler wondered if anyone was home. Finally a maid appeared in the doorway.

"Can you spare some food?" the traveler asked her. "I have been traveling for days and am very hungry."

"I'm sorry, but I have only a few potatoes," the maid said sadly. "There's not enough to spare or share. Why don't you try my neighbor next door?"

"I already have," said the hungry traveler, "but he was grumpy and just slammed the door."

The traveler thanked the maid and moved on. "It looks like finding some food in this village will be more difficult than I had hoped," he thought as his tummy grumbled.

The traveler visited every house in the village, but no one had enough food to spare. One house had only cabbage, the next had only carrots, and a third had only salt and pepper.

The hungry traveler found that no one had food to spare, and he decided to move on. Before he got very far, he stopped to rest in the shade of a tree just outside the village.

"It's a shame," he thought, "such a nice village and such a beautiful day, but nobody is outdoors playing or talking with each other."

The traveler reached into his bag and found the stone. It gave him a brilliant idea, and he headed back to the town.

"Come out of your houses, everybody!" shouted the hungry traveler. "I have a magic stone. It will give us enough food for a wonderful meal. Everyone in town will have plenty to eat, and there will even be enough left over to spare and share!"

One by one, the curious villagers peeked out of their doors and windows.

The grumpy villager who slammed the door on the traveler earlier looked out of his window and grumbled, "What's all the racket about?"

"Come help me make a pot of delicious stone soup," the traveler replied.

The maid stepped out of her house to see what the hungry traveler was up to.

"Does anybody have a large soup kettle to get us started?" the traveler asked.

"I've got one that you can use," said the grumpy villager, "but I don't think it will do any good. I don't think your magic stone will really work."

Most of the villagers were excited, but some felt the same way as the grumpy villager.

"Do you really believe he can make soup from a stone?" asked one young lady.

"I guess we'll find out soon," said another. "I certainly hope he can. I haven't had good soup in a long time."

The grumpy villager brought his large kettle and placed it on a pile of sticks for the fire. "Let's see if that magic stone of yours can really make enough soup for all of us."

"Don't worry," said the traveler. "There will be plenty."

The hungry traveler placed the smooth, oval stone into the kettle of water and began to stir. After a little while he tasted the soup.

"Not bad," he said, "but I think it could use a little salt and pepper."

"I've got some," said one of the young ladies. "I'll run home and get it."

"Perhaps the soup would taste even better if I shared my potatoes," the maid suggested.

"Yes, that's an excellent idea," said the traveler. "Why don't you go and get them, and we'll add them to the kettle right away."

The young lady returned and sprinkled her salt and pepper into the kettle. Then the maid came back and dropped in her potatoes. Once again the traveler stirred the stone soup. When he tasted it for the second time, all the villagers watched him with anticipation.

"This is very good, but it would taste even better with some carrots and cabbage," said the traveler.

A young boy ran home to get some carrots, and a little girl ran home to get some cabbage.

By now, everyone was having so much fun spending time together that they forgot how hungry they were. Even the grumpy villager was no longer grumpy.

"Let's turn this meal into a party!" he shouted.

The girl returned with her cabbage, and the boy soon followed with his carrots.

"Just think, a huge kettle of soup made from a magic stone," said the boy as he dropped his carrots into the kettle. "I can't wait to try it!"

"Neither can I," said the girl, as she added her cabbage to the soup.

Finally the hungry traveler announced that the stone soup was ready. He filled all the bowls, and the villagers began to eat together.

Afterward there was plenty of soup left over.

"There's enough to spare and share!" said the young lady.

The villagers were so happy after dinner that they didn't want the evening to end. They played music together and danced with one another. The village was alive with chatter and laughter for the first time in a long time.

"I didn't know you could play the banjo so well," the maid said to the no-longer-grumpy villager.

"And I didn't know you could play the washboard so well," he responded with a smile. "We make an excellent band when we play together!"

"I think there was a lot we didn't know about each other until that traveler came along," said the maid.

The next morning, the traveler said good-bye to his new friends. The villagers were sad to see him leave after he had brought out so much good in all of them.

"I want you to have this," he said as he handed the smooth, oval stone to the villagers. "Now you will always be able to make stone soup together, and you will never be hungry or sad or grumpy again."

Each of the villagers hugged the traveler and told him to come back and visit soon.

As the no-longer-hungry traveler headed out of the lovely little village, he stumbled over another stone in the road. He picked it up at once and admired its dark, jagged edges. The traveler looked at the stone carefully and finally decided to keep it.

"You never know when a stone like this might come in handy," he said to himself as he placed it in his bag.

Snips and Snails

Illustrated by Marina Fedotova

What are little boys made of, made of?
What are little boys made of?
Snips and snails and puppy-dog tails,
that's what little boys are made of.

Sugar and Spice

Illustrated by Marina Fedotova

What are little girls made of, made of?
What are little girls made of?
Sugar and spice, and all things nice,
that's what little girls are made of.

Twinkle, Twinkle, Little Star

Illustrated by Dubravka Kolanovic

Twinkle was a little star. His mother was a Get Well Star. His father was a Safe Journey Star. Twinkle hoped that when he grew up, he would have an important star job, just like his parents.

Mama Star said, "You will be a big star soon enough, Twinkle."

Papa Star said, "One day you will find the perfect job."

Twinkle hoped his parents were right. With a sparkly spin, he waved good-bye and went out exploring on his own.

Twinkle wondered
if he could be a First
Day of School Star.
"I would help the
children be brave and make friends.
I would even help them with their ABCs and 123s!"
said Twinkle. "Being a First Day of School Star would
certainly be an important job."

Twinkle thought about being a Tie Your Shoes Star.
"I would help children learn which is left and which is
right, and teach them to make extra-
tight knots and bows," said
Twinkle. "I would help
children to not skin their
knees! Yes, if I were a Tie
Your Shoes Star, I would
be very important."

Twinkle considered being a Learn to Swim Star.

"If I were a Learn to Swim Star, I would help children kick and paddle in the water," said Twinkle. "I would help them learn to blow bubbles and breathe under water as they swim! I could do a lot of good being a Learn to Swim Star."

Twinkle also thought he could go far as a Ride a Bike Star.

"I would help children steer straight and avoid the busy streets," he said. "I could also help to remind them to always wear a helmet. Safety is certainly very important."

One night, as Twinkle
sparkled in the sky, a little boy
said, "Look, Mama! I think that star is
twinkling just for me! I will make a wish on that star."
Then the little boy closed his eyes tight, and he
wished to make a friend.

"Mama! Papa!" cried
Twinkle. "I heard a little boy
wish for a friend!"

Mama Star and Papa Star
smiled. "It sounds like you are
a Wishing Star, Twinkle."

Twinkle sparkled brightly
over the little wishing boy.

54

"To make a friend, you must look for someone who needs a friend, too," Twinkle told the little boy. "Just smile and say *hello*. Share a toy. Be nice. But most important of all, be yourself."

Twinkle grew up to be the best Wishing Star. He even has his very own song:

> *Twinkle, twinkle, little star,*
>> *how I wonder what you are.*
> *Up above the world so high,*
>> *like a diamond in the sky,*
> *Twinkle, twinkle, little star,*
>> *how I wonder what you are!*

Twelve Dancing Princesses

Adapted by Michael P. Fertig
Illustrated by Jeffrey Ebbeler

Once upon a time in a faraway kingdom, there lived a king who had twelve daughters. To say that having twelve daughters was a handful would be unfair to the king, for it was far more than that. The king was a very protective father, and he worried about his princesses. Also, he did not always understand their ways.

Each night, the king carefully closed the door to his daughters' bedroom. Yet, each morning, he found the princesses tired and out of sorts. More puzzling still, every morning he found their new pairs of silk dancing slippers worn to shreds.

When the king asked his daughters about this, they would laugh and say, "Don't be silly, Father. We go to sleep each night and sleep soundly until the morning."

But the king was not convinced. He decided to offer a reward to any person from his kingdom who could solve this mystery.

The next day, one of the king's
subjects—a man called
Rawling—was out walking in the
countryside. He was a poor but clever
man, and he liked to walk and think.
He had just stopped to eat his
modest lunch when a
strange little woman
came hobbling by.

"Good day, madam," said Rawling, standing to greet her. "Would you care for some lunch?"

"Thank you," said the old woman. "You are very kind to share with me, especially when you have so little."

In return, the old woman gave Rawling a cloak that could make him invisible. "Take this to the castle," she said. "If you are clever enough, you can use it to claim the king's reward. But remember, if the princesses offer you a drink, do not drink it, or the cloak will be useless to you."

Rawling thanked the old woman for the cloak and the advice. Then he finished his meal and set off for the castle.

When Rawling arrived, the king was eager to see if *this* young man could succeed in solving the mystery. Several others had already tried and failed.

"Welcome," said the king. "Please make yourself at home while you solve my mystery."

When Rawling met the princesses, they offered him a goblet of punch.

"Thank you," said Rawling. But he remembered what the kind old woman had said. When the princesses turned away, Rawling poured the punch under the table without drinking a drop.

Rawling pretended to yawn. He was then shown to his bed, where he pretended to fall asleep.

"It is safe now," said the eldest princess. "Thanks to what we put in his goblet, he will sleep soundly until the morning, just like all the others did."

With that, she tapped three times on her bedpost. The bed rose from the floor, revealing a secret staircase. The princesses eagerly ran down the winding stairs.

Rawling put on his magic cloak and followed. As he caught up with the princesses, he accidentally stepped on the gown of the youngest princess. She was startled, but could see no one when she turned around.

Even so, Rawling thought he saw a twinkle in her eye and a smile on her face.

At the bottom of the stairs was an enchanted forest along the edge of a lake. The trees had branches with leaves of gold and silver and diamonds. Rawling had never seen anything like it in all his life. He plucked one bough from each type of twinkling tree, and tucked them safely into his cloak.

Twelve princes met the princesses and guided them to boats. They began to row across the lake to a beautiful castle. Rawling snuck onto the boat carrying the youngest princess.

The prince who rowed the boat thought it seemed heavier than usual.

"You row more slowly tonight," Rawling heard the young princess tell the prince. "I am enjoying the change." This time Rawling was sure he saw the young princess's eyes sparkle when she looked in his direction.

The twelve princesses and the twelve princes walked arm in arm into a grand ballroom within the castle.

Rawling crept softly behind, marveling at all that he found there. Beautiful music seemed to float from the ceilings. Clusters of candles hung in the air, casting the softest of glows. The wonderful room was most certainly enchanted.

The princesses and princes danced around the ballroom. Rawling watched as each pair moved more gracefully than the last.

The couples danced for hours, pausing only to sip punch from golden goblets. They sipped from the goblets all night long, and yet the goblets were always full. At last, the princes escorted the twelve princesses back to the secret staircase.

The twelve princesses were tired from their evening of dancing so they walked slowly. Rawling was able to hurry ahead of them and slip back into his bed before they returned.

The youngest princess peeked in on him. "Our handsome guest is sleeping as though he's lived a thousand lives," she told her sisters.

With that, the princesses removed their tattered dancing slippers and placed them in a row. Then they climbed into their own beds and fell asleep.

The next morning, Rawling crept out of bed and went to find the king. He carried with him proof of all he had seen the night before.

"Your Majesty," said Rawling,
"I have solved your riddle. It seems
that your lovely daughters have been
wearing out their slippers by dancing all
night long." And he told the king about the
enchanted events of the evening.

The king listened intently. "Can you produce
proof of this story?" he asked. Rawling presented
the king with a golden goblet.

"This, Your Majesty, is a goblet from the
enchanted castle where your daughters dance
all night," Rawling said. "I ask you to put your lips
to it and take a sip."

"This goblet is empty," said the king. But once
he raised the goblet to his lips, it instantly filled
with punch.

"How is this possible?" asked the king.

"The goblet is enchanted, just like the forest and the castle," said Rawling.

Rawling then laid out the three twinkling tree branches. One had leaves of silver, one had leaves of gold, and the last had leaves of diamonds.

"These are from the forest near the enchanted castle," Rawling explained. "But the greatest proof of my tale must come directly from your daughters."

The princesses, who were listening at the door, confirmed what Rawling had said. They apologized to their father for being dishonest with him.

The king was pleased. "You have solved this great mystery," he said. "And you have given up a great fortune to present me with proof, as well. I owe you a great reward. You may have anything you would like."

"Your Majesty," spoke Rawling, "in my brief time with your daughters, I have grown fond of your youngest. She is as beautiful as she is clever." Rawling looked at the young princess. "If she will agree, I would like to ask for her hand in marriage."

The young princess smiled and her eye twinkled. She had been charmed by the brave and clever man. The king granted Rawling's request, and the princess eagerly agreed to marry him.

The pair lived—and danced—happily ever after.

71

Harmony Farm

Adapted by Mary Rowitz
Illustrated by Sharron O'Neil

One day on a farm called Harmony, Cow looked at Hen curiously.

"Hen," she said, "what is it like to lay an egg?"

"It's nice," replied Hen. "The farmer is always happy when he sees a new egg in my nest."

"I thought so," replied Cow. "It looks very exciting. I think I'd like to try it."

All of the animals stopped and stared at Cow.

"What do you mean, Cow?" asked Cat.

"Don't any of you wonder what it would be like to try something new?" asked Cow. "I am tired of making the milk each day!"

The animals all confessed that they might like a change. Soon all of the animals decided to trade jobs— all except Pig. He was busy eating.

Suddenly Hen cried, "Oh no! We forgot about Pig!"

The animals all walked over to the sty to break the news to Pig. They felt terrible.

"Pig, I'm sorry, but we all decided to try new jobs on the farm," said Cow.

"But in all the excitement," said Cat, "we forgot to ask what you would like to try, and now there aren't any new jobs left."

Pig let out a sigh of relief. "Thank goodness!" he exclaimed. "I was afraid you were going to ask me to chase mice."

"But Pig," said Hen, "don't you get bored just eating and rolling around in the mud all day?"

"No, never!" replied Pig. "I'm really good at what I do. I can eat slop like nobody's business. And at the end of the day, that feels very rewarding."

"But wouldn't you like to try something different?" asked Sheepdog. "Like herding the sheep?"

"Goodness, no!" replied Pig. "I have a great life. But thank you for the offer. I wish you all the best of luck."

Once they were satisfied that Pig's feelings were not hurt, all of the animals left to begin their new jobs— all except Pig.

"Cow, what am I doing wrong?" Hen asked, a bit embarrassed that the milk pail was still empty after she had been sitting on it for a while.

"I was just wondering the same thing," said Cow. "I have been sitting on this nest for quite some time and haven't laid a single egg!"

"The sheep just don't respect me," said Donkey as he chased after the sheep.

"How do you pull this plow?" Sheepdog wondered.

"If you think the plow is heavy," said Cat, "try the wagon! Sheesh!"

"And those mice are fast little ones!" chimed in Horse. "I couldn't catch a single one."

Soon all of the animals discovered they weren't having much luck with their jobs—all except Pig.

Pig watched his friends. They looked so unhappy that he decided to find out what had happened. The animals all told Pig how they had failed at their new jobs.

"Friends," said Pig, "don't think about what you can't do. Think about what you can do!"

Pig reminded his friends of their unique talents. The animals felt better and were happy to go back to their old ways. They all felt thankful that they had jobs they could do well.

But they were also glad they had tried something new. They laughed, clucked, mooed, brayed, barked, meowed, neighed, and oinked about it for many years to come.

Baby Bluebird

Illustrated by John Kanzler

Baby Bluebird looked in the sky one day. She saw the other birds flying. "I should be flying, too," she said, "but I don't know how."

Her friend Rabbit saw the birds flying as well, and wanted to help. "Flying looks a lot like hopping," said Rabbit. "If you hop high enough, you might start to fly."

Baby Bluebird decided to try hopping. She jumped into the air but soon came back down to the ground. She tried again and again.

"Well," asked Rabbit, "is hopping like flying?"

"It's a little like flying," Baby Bluebird said. "But I keep landing. I don't think flying is supposed to be this bouncy."

Gopher had been watching Baby Bluebird hop and wanted to help her.

"It seems to me," said Gopher, "that flying is a lot like digging. Maybe if you practice digging with me, it will help you learn to flap your wings and fly."

"I'll give it a try," said Baby Bluebird.

She found a nice patch of dirt. She flapped her wings, trying to dig a hole. Flapping in the dirt did not help Baby Bluebird learn to fly, but it did raise a huge cloud of dust.

"I don't think flying is supposed to be this dusty," Baby Bluebird said with a cough. "I don't know if I'll ever learn to fly."

Turtle heard Baby Bluebird and wanted to help her fly, too.

"Flying looks a little like swimming," Turtle said. "Maybe if you practice swimming through the water with me, it will help you learn to glide through the air. Hop in!"

So Baby Bluebird dove into the water and tried to paddle and glide alongside Turtle.

"Oh, my! It's so wet!" she cried as she splashed and spluttered in the water. "I don't think flying is supposed to be this soggy."

Baby Bluebird flapped her wings to dry them off. "It's no use," she said sadly. "I'll never learn to fly. I might as well stop trying."

"You must never stop trying," said Turtle. "If you want to fly, you will find a way."

87

Baby Bluebird sat and thought. "Swimming didn't work," she said. "And neither did hopping or digging. But I think I know what I need to do."

Baby Bluebird took a running start. She hopped like Rabbit. She flapped her wings like Gopher digging. And once she was in the air, she glided like Turtle swimming.

"I'm flying!" Baby Bluebird chirped. She lifted her head and began to sing. It was the happiest song the animals had ever heard.

Answer to a Child's Question

Illustrated by Marina Fedotova

Do you ask what the birds say? The robin, the dove,
    the linnet, and thrush say, "I love and I love!"
In the winter they are silent—the wind is so strong;
    what *it* says, I don't know, but it sings a loud song.
Then green leaves, and blossoms, and sunny warm weather,
    and singing and loving all come back together.
Now the lark is so brimful of gladness and love,
    the green fields below, and the blue sky above,
That it sings, and it sings, and forever sings free:
    "I love my love, and my love loves me."

The Elves and the Shoemaker

Adapted by Sylvia Vanerka
Illustrated by Jon Goodell

Many winters ago, in a small, prosperous village not far away, there lived a shoemaker and his wife. For many years they earned a good living making shoes for the people of the town.

It was common knowledge among the villagers that the fine shoes bought from the shoemaker's shop were sure to last a long, long time. And they tended to be stylish, as well. The little shop was always busy and bustling, and the villagers were always satisfied with their shoes. All of this changed, however, after one winter storm.

It was the fiercest snowstorm anyone had ever seen. And when the spring thaw came, the melted snow flooded every farm for miles around.

The ruined farmland caused many people to move away. As more and more people left the village, the shoemaker and his wife sold fewer and fewer shoes. Soon they were down to their last piece of leather. It would be enough to make only one more pair. After that, they did not know what they would do.

Just as the shoemaker was about to cut the leather to make the final pair of shoes, he realized how late it was. With a yawn, he set his tools and the piece of leather on his workbench and went to bed.

The next morning, the shoemaker and his wife came down to the workshop to find a surprise. On his bench sat the finest pair of shoes they had ever seen. The shoemaker rubbed his eyes in astonishment.

"My dear," he said to his wife, "did you make these fine shoes during the night?"

"No," she replied, "I did not."

"Well, I did not either," he said. "I wonder who did?"

Before his wife could even shrug, the bell on their shop door rang. A customer entered.

"Hello, good sir and madam," said a well-dressed man. "I am visiting from the city and have stepped in a very large mud puddle. My shoes are decidedly ruined. Do you have anything in my size?"

The shoemaker's wife grabbed the mysterious pair of shoes from the workbench and slid them onto the feet of the well-dressed man. They fit perfectly!

"I say," said the man, "this might be the best-looking pair of shoes I have ever seen or worn! And they are certainly the most comfortable."

97

So pleased was he with the shoes that the well-dressed man paid the shoemaker with a full gold coin.

The gold coin was enough for the shoemaker to buy leather for two new pairs of shoes. Once again, he left the leather and his tools on his workbench and went to bed.

The next morning, the shoemaker and his wife came down to the shop to discover that two more pairs of shoes had been made from the leather he left out.

"How could this be?" the shoemaker asked his wife.

Before she could answer, two ladies walked in.

"Good day," one of them said. "My husband came in here yesterday and bought the most exquisite pair of shoes. My sister and I would each like a pair as well."

As luck had it, the two new pairs of shoes fit them perfectly.

"Goodness," said the sister, "these are delightful! I'll tell everyone I know to visit your shop."

And she did. Soon, the shop was bustling again. The two women—and their many friends—paid handsomely for their shoes. The shoemaker and his wife were able to buy more and more leather. And night after night, the leather was sewn into fine pairs of shoes.

"We must discover who is helping us," the shoemaker said to his wife one evening. "Let's stay up late to find out."

The shoemaker and his wife sat quietly in the shadows of their shop. Just after midnight, they heard a sound. They peered around a corner and spied two tiny elves happily at work on a new pair of shoes.

"Why, it's elves!" whispered the shoemaker's wife. "But look at their clothes. They work so hard to make such fine shoes for us, yet they wear only rags themselves."

The shoemaker's wife decided that she would sew new suits for the elves to thank them for all their hard work.

The next day was another busy one in the shop. The shoemaker and his wife had enough shoes to fill every shelf. At the end of the day, the shoemaker's wife left out two tiny outfits. She hoped the elves would like them.

Then the shoemaker and his wife hid. Once again, they heard a sound just after midnight. When they peered around the corner this time, they saw the two tiny elves wearing their new clothes and dancing happily together.

After that night, the elves never returned. But the town was thriving again, due in part to the success of the shoemaker's shop. People traveled for miles to buy shoes there. Times were good again. The shoemaker and his wife lived happily ever after, thanks to the kindness of two tiny strangers.

What Do You Call Her?

Written by Gale Greenlee
Illustrated by Angela Jarecki

What do you call your grandma?
Is she Meemaw or Mamoo?
Do you call her Gram or Granny?
Mim or Pitty Poo?

Jalen calls his gram Miss Shuga,
because she smells so sweet.
To Betty, she's Creek Momma,
because she lives behind the creek.

Maria calls her gram Abuela,
or sometimes just Abu.
Boris calls his gram Babushka,
and Kim likes Ludie Loo.

In China, she is Nai Nai;
    in Swahili, she's Sho Sho.
Some folks say Nyanya,
    and in Creole she's Go Go.

But it really doesn't matter
    what name you know her by.
You can call her Queenie, Babs, or Tati,
    or even Miss Moon Pie!

She could be your Ya Ya,
    your Nonnie or Nanoo;
Whatever name you call her,
    she's full of love for you.

A Story for Squeakins

Illustrated by Teri Weidner

It was time for little Squeakins to take his afternoon nap, so he asked Granny Mouse to read him a story. Stories always helped Squeakins fall asleep.

"All right then, dearest dear," said Granny. "What kind of a story would you like to hear?"

"A nice one, with a happy ending," answered little Squeakins.

So Granny went to fetch the happiest-ending storybook she could find. But on her way to the library, she ran into a bit of trouble. Mean Mittens the cat was guarding the door.

"Hello, Granny," said Mean Mittens. "What a nice treat you'd be to eat."

"Oh, no! You must let me pass," said Granny Mouse. "I must fetch a happy-ending story to read to Squeakins before his nap."

"Well," said Mean Mittens, "I'll let you pass if you promise to bring me fresh milk from the cow."

So Granny scurried straight to Brown
Bessie to ask for some milk.

"Brown Bessie, may I please have some
milk to give to Mean Mittens so
I can find a storybook?"

Brown Bessie was happy
to help. "I promise to
give you milk if you
can find me a shiny
new cowbell
to wear."

So Granny Mouse scurried straight to Tinker Tom to ask him for a shiny new cowbell.

"Tinker Tom, may I please have a shiny new cowbell for Brown Bessie?" asked Granny Mouse. "I must fetch a happy storybook for Squeakins!"

"I will give you a cowbell if you make me a glass of lemonade," said Tinker Tom.

So Granny scurried off to Leafy Lemon Tree to ask for some lemons to make lemonade.

"Leafy Lemon Tree, may I please have some lemons to make a glass of lemonade for Tinker Tom so he will give Brown Bessie a shiny new cowbell so that she will give fresh milk to Mean Mittens so I can pass? I must find a happy story to read to little Squeakins."

"I'll give you as many lemons as you like," said Leafy Lemon Tree, "if you can find some water to sprinkle on me."

So Granny Mouse stood in the middle of the yard and talked to the clouds.

"Puffy, fluffy clouds, may I please have some water to sprinkle on Leafy Lemon Tree so he will give me lemons to make lemonade for Tinker Tom…"

Granny took a breath. "So that
Tinker Tom will give me a shiny
new cowbell for Brown Bessie
so that she will give me some
fresh milk for Mean Mittens
so that I can pass? Because
I must fetch the happiest
of happy-ending
storybooks to read
to little Squeakins!"

And the puffy, fluffy clouds answered Granny Mouse with a big BOOM!

The clouds gave water.

Leafy Lemon Tree gave lemons.

Tinker Tom gave a cowbell.

Brown Bessie gave milk.

And Mean Mittens let Granny pass.

Finally, Granny was able to fetch the happiest-ending storybook that she could find to read to her little Squeakins.

But by the time Granny Mouse got back…

...Squeakins was already asleep!

A Baby Is Born

Written by Melanie Zanoza Bartelme
Illustrated by Steve Whitlow

A baby is born
at the top of a tree.

A baby is born
underneath the blue sea.

A baby is born
in the dewy, green glen.

A baby is born
in a cozy, warm den.

A baby is born
in a bed of soft hay.

A baby is born
and then tucked away.

In deserts, on snowbanks,
    and under the seas,
On mountains, in valleys,
    and in tops of trees,
All over the world,
    every night and each day,
A baby is born
    special in its own way!

The Princess and the Pea

Adapted by Michael P. Fertig
Illustrated by Anthony Lewis

In a land so far away that it would take as long to travel there from one direction as from any other, there lived a young prince named Horatio. Prince Horatio was much admired for being kind and loyal, as well as smart, brave, and handsome. In short, he was the perfect prince. And as if that were not enough, he was also quite a stylish dresser.

All of the ladies of the land wanted to marry Prince Horatio. It was well known throughout his kingdom that the prince was searching for a bride. And it was also well known that his mother was very particular about whom she would allow her son to marry. Any woman who wished to wed Prince Horatio must be a princess, through and through.

"There are so many princesses these days," said the prince's mother. "Only a real princess with a kind, generous, and delicate nature will be good enough for my dear Horatio."

The prince was bothered by his mother's wish for him to find the perfect bride. But in truth, none of the princesses he had met were that interesting to him. He simply had not yet met the princess of his dreams.

One particular dark and rainy evening, however, all of that was about to change. The prince was just getting ready to turn in for the night when there was a knock at the castle door.

"Forgive me for the intrusion," said a lovely young woman, "but my carriage has lost a wheel in the road. May I impose upon you for shelter this evening?"

"Of course," replied the prince. "Please come in."

"Thank you very much," she said. "My name is Astrid. I am a princess from Wainscott, just over the hills."

The prince led Princess Astrid to the castle's parlor where a fire was burning in the hearth, and the two sat down together. They immediately fell into conversation and talked well into the night. Before they realized it, the prince and the princess were holding hands.

Elsewhere in the castle, the prince's mother had devised a plan to determine whether Astrid was really a princess. It is a little-known fact that a real princess has such a sensitive nature that she can detect even the slightest flaw in otherwise comfortable sleeping arrangements. So the queen hid a single uncooked pea under a stack of twenty of the softest mattresses in the kingdom. A true princess—one who met the queen's standards—would certainly be able to feel the pea.

Astrid was shown to her room. She climbed atop the twenty mattresses, hoping to dream of Prince Horatio. But sleep would not come.

Aware that something was not right, Astrid climbed down and slipped her arm under the bottom mattress. She pulled out the pea and said, "Aha! Just as I thought. Now for some rest."

In the morning, the queen asked Astrid how she had slept.

"I was quite uncomfortable at first," Astrid admitted. "But then I discovered a pea under the mattresses. After I removed it, I slept very well, thank you."

The prince and his mother exchanged glances.

In a flash, Prince Horatio was on his knee, proposing to beautiful Princess Astrid. Much to the dismay of the unwed ladies of the kingdom, Princess Astrid accepted. The couple remains happily married to this very day.

The Quarrelsome Kittens

Two little kittens, one stormy night,
   began to quarrel, began to fight;
One had a mouse, the other had none—
   that's the way the quarrel had begun.

"I'll have that mouse," said the bigger cat.
   "You'll have that mouse? We'll see about that!"
"I will have that mouse," said the elder one.
   Said the younger, "Of course, after I'm done."

129

I mentioned it was on a stormy night
    when these two kittens began to fight;
Well, the old woman seized her bristly broom,
    and swept those two kittens right out of the room.

The ground was covered with frost and snow,
    and the two little kittens had nowhere to go;
So they lay down on the mat at the door,
    while the old woman finished sweeping the floor.

Then they crept in, as quiet as mice,
    all wet with snow, and as cold as ice;
For they found it was better, that stormy night,
    to lie down and sleep than to quarrel and fight.

Big Bunny Family

Original story written by Lora Kalkman
Illustrated by Margie Moore

Benny Bunny lived with his big bunny family in a cozy home in the forest. The special thing about Benny's family was that he had more brothers and sisters than you can count on all of your fingers and all of your toes. Benny was the oldest.

Benny felt crowded in his cozy forest home. No matter where he went, his brothers and sisters were always close by him. Some days Benny had to squeeze onto the sofa or even sit on the floor. Some nights he had to sleep on the very edge of the bed.

"There just isn't enough room for me," Benny sighed.

Benny also felt tired of sharing. He always had to share his toys—even his favorite bouncy ball. Sometimes Benny also had to share his carrots at dinner.

"I never get to have anything for myself around here!" grumbled Benny.

Early one morning, Benny's littlest sister rolled over and pushed him out of the bed.

"That's the last straw!" Benny said. "I am going to go off on my own and find a new home."

That day, Benny went to the kitchen to pack some carrots for the trip. As he worked, he thought about his new life.

"I will finally have some peace and quiet," Benny thought happily. "I will have all the room I need, I won't have to share my toys, and I can eat as many carrots as I want."

On his way out, Benny picked up his favorite ball to bring along. Then he glanced around his cozy home one last time. His brothers and sisters were all busy hopping and talking and making a lot of noise.

"I'll bet they won't even notice I'm gone," Benny thought.

Then he set off alone.

Hopping down the bunny trail, Benny soon reached the other side of the forest. He came upon a lovely meadow where there were no other bunnies in sight.

"This will be perfect!" he said to himself. He sat down to enjoy some peace and quiet, all on his own.

Before long, Benny began to feel bored. He decided to play ball. He bounced his ball up and down. He tossed his ball in the air and caught it.

At first, Benny thought this was wonderful. For the first time that he could remember, there were no other bunnies to get in his way! But when Benny threw his ball, there was no one else to catch it, and when he kicked his ball, there was no one else to chase after it.

Finally, Benny put the ball away and decided it was time to eat dinner.

Sitting down to eat alone, Benny arranged his carrots neatly. Finally, he could have all his carrots without sharing any! But then Benny realized there were too many carrots for him to eat all by himself.

Seeing the uneaten carrots made Benny think about his brothers and sisters. He wondered if they were hungry. A tear fell from Benny's eye.

Benny missed his big bunny family. He missed his cozy home, he missed sharing his ball, and he even missed sharing his carrots with his younger sisters and brothers.

Benny decided that the empty meadow was not the home for him. He packed up all of his things and set out along the bunny trail once more—this time in the direction of his crowded, cozy home!

When Benny rounded the bend, he saw his entire big bunny family gathered outside.

All of Benny's brothers and sisters came running toward him. Benny smiled. His big bunny family *had* noticed he was gone, and they missed him. They had all been very worried.

Benny felt bad for making his family worry.

"I thought I wanted to live by myself," Benny explained, "but I missed all of you so much. I promise I will never go away on my own again."

That night, Benny played ball with his brothers and sisters. He didn't mind squeezing onto the sofa. He was even happy to share his carrots with his brothers and sisters.

"I love sharing this cozy home with my big bunny family," Benny declared. "I think I am the luckiest bunny in the whole wide world."

The Owl and the Pussycat

Original poem written by Edward Lear

The Owl and the Pussycat went to sea
in a beautiful pea-green boat:
They took some honey, and plenty of money,
wrapped up in a five-pound note.

The Owl looked up to the stars above,
and sang with a small guitar,
"Oh lovely Kitty, oh Kitty, my love,
what a beautiful kitty you are!"

Kitty said to the Owl, "You elegant fowl,
   how charmingly sweet you sing!"
"Let us be married; too long we have tarried!"
   said the Owl as he gave her a ring.

They dined on mince and slices of quince,
   which they ate with a runcible spoon;
And hand in hand, on the edge of the sand,
   they danced by the light of the moon.

Little Kitty

Illustrated by Lisa Alderson

I like little kitty,
   her coat is so warm,
And if I don't tease her,
   she'll do me no harm;
So I'll not pull her tail,
   nor drive her away,
But Kitty and I
   very gently will play.

The Velveteen Rabbit

Adaped by Amy Adair
Illustrated by Teddy Edinjiklian

One Christmas morning, a little boy found a special gift in his stocking. It was a velveteen rabbit. The little boy loved the velveteen rabbit! He tucked the rabbit under his arm while he opened the rest of his gifts. The little boy put the rabbit in his bedroom with all of his other toys. Some toys were shiny and others made noise. Some toys even had batteries on the inside.

The velveteen rabbit
felt plain next to the other
toys. He was just fabric and
stiches, with fluff inside!

The velveteen rabbit became
friends with a shabby old horse. The
little boy had played with the horse so much
that one of her ears was hanging on with a pin.

"Flashy toys don't last," said the horse. "They
only have batteries inside, nothing lovable. They
will never be real."

"How do I become real?" asked the
velveteen rabbit.

"You become real after someone
loves you for a long time," replied
the old horse.

"You may be old and tattered," the horse continued, "but that's all right. When you are loved, you are truly beautiful!"

The velveteen rabbit wanted to be real.

That night, the little boy chose the velveteen rabbit to sleep with him. The velveteen rabbit snuggled up close to the boy. From then on, the velveteen rabbit was always with the little boy, wherever he went. They went on picnics, they walked in the woods, and they played in the garden.

The velveteen rabbit's heart was full of joy. He loved the boy and felt lucky to spend so much time with him. The velveteen rabbit was so happy on the inside that he didn't notice how shabby he had become on the outside.

One afternoon, the little boy and the velveteen rabbit were playing in the garden. Suddenly, lightning flashed in the sky and it began to rain. The little boy ran straight home and forgot the velveteen rabbit in the garden.

The rabbit was all alone and felt very sad. He missed the little boy.

At bedtime, the little boy realized the velveteen rabbit was still outside. He looked up at his mother with big, sad eyes.

"May I please go rescue my friend, the velveteen rabbit?" asked the little boy. "I know it is dark and rainy out, but my friend needs me."

His mother nodded and found him a light. He searched in the darkness until he found the poor, very wet rabbit. The boy tucked the rabbit under his arm and ran inside.

"Please be careful where you leave your toys," said the little boy's mother as she dried him with a warm towel.

"My rabbit is not a toy!" said the boy. "He is my real friend."

The velveteen rabbit was cold, and his fur was dripping with water, but he didn't mind at all. He was happy that the little boy had thought of him as a friend.

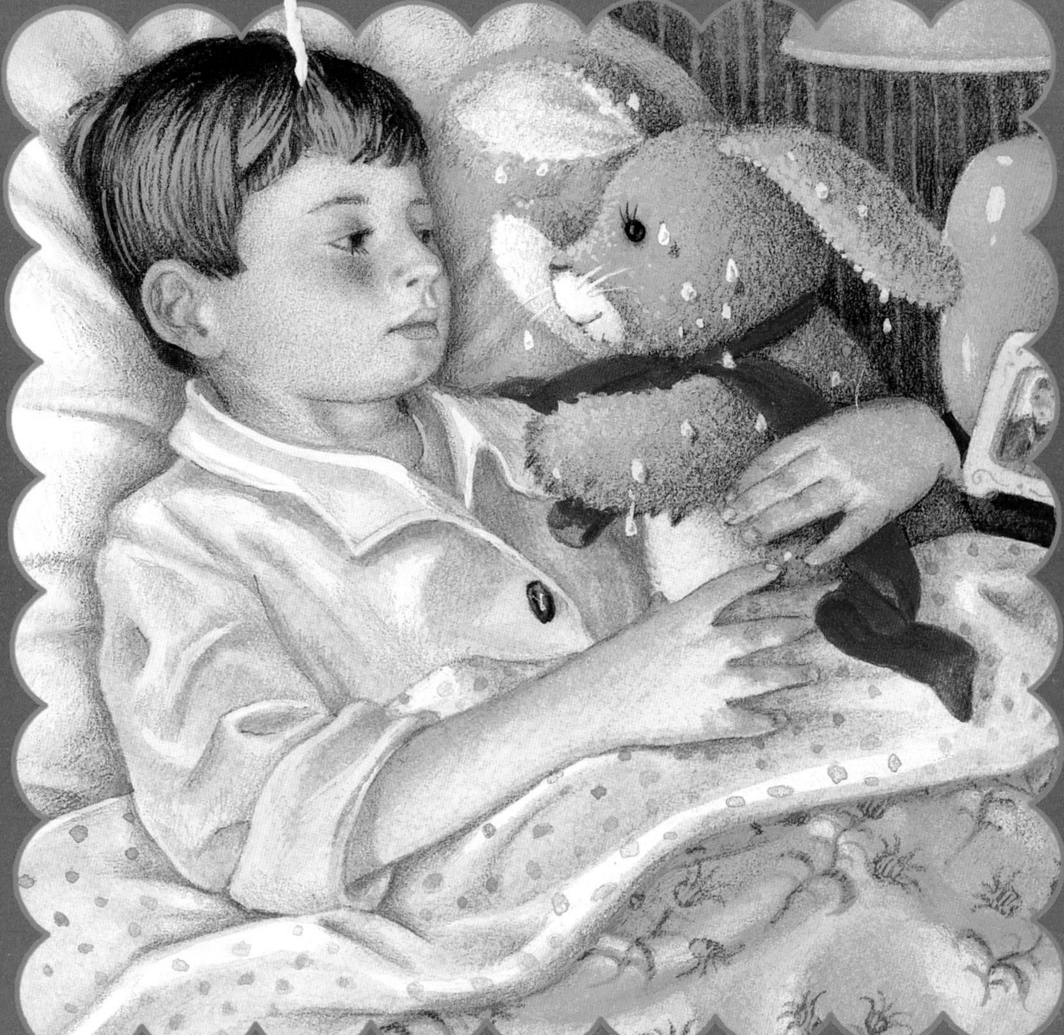

At the end of that summer, the little boy's family was going on a long trip. The velveteen rabbit was excited for another adventure with the little boy. But then they drove away. The little boy had forgotten to pack the velveteen rabbit.

The velveteen rabbit began to cry. His teardrops rolled off his fluffy cheek and fell to the ground. In the spot where his tears fell, a beautiful, magical flower began to grow. When the flower bloomed, there was a fairy tucked inside the petals. She stood up and stretched her wings.

"Hello, dear rabbit," she said sweetly. "Your love for the little boy has earned you the right to become real."

"But aren't I real already?" asked the velveteen rabbit.

"Only to the boy," explained the fairy. "Now I will make you real to the whole world!"

With a wink and a wave of her wand, the fairy changed the velveteen rabbit into a real rabbit.

The rabbit blinked his eyes. Then he took a little hop, and hopped again, and again! He jumped over flowers and rocks. He played with other rabbits in the woods. He nibbled on lettuce from the garden. He felt wonderful.

When the little boy returned from his long trip, he ran to the woods to play. He met a rabbit that looked very familiar. The rabbit wasn't like all the other rabbits in the woods, which quickly hopped away when they saw the boy.

This rabbit hopped right up to the boy, as if to say, "Hello." The boy knelt down and smiled at the friendly rabbit. "You remind me of my old friend, the velveteen rabbit," said the little boy. "Do you think we could be friends?"

The rabbit wiggled his little nose, and the little boy laughed.

The rabbit loved hopping over rocks and flowers. He loved playing with other rabbits in the woods. And he loved the little boy, whose love and friendship had made him real.

157

The Brown Thrush

There's a merry brown thrush
   sitting up in a tree.
She's singing to me! She's singing to me!
   And what does she say, little girl, little boy?

"Oh, the world's running over with joy!
   Don't you hear? Don't you see?
Hush! Look! Up in my tree,
   I'm as happy as can be!"